# *Salvation*

## *and the*

# SOUNDNESS
# OF MIND

MIRIAM WHITEHEAD

Broad Wing Press
Capital Heights, MD

ISBN: ISBN: 978-1-938373-53-4
LCCN: 2021938084

# Table of Contents

Preface................................................ii

Writing in the Dark................................1

Labels ............................................. 5

Lying/Masking................................... 11

Rules vs Relationship.........................19

Those Caves and Islands............................ 33

Islands....................................... 39

Life from A to V............................... 47

Footstools....................................77

Take Up Thy Bed and Walk ........................ 81

New Garment................................. 87

## Dedication

This book is dedicated to those who
seek a sound mind.

**\*It is okay to read this book
multiple times.**

# Preface

I pray this book would increase your prayer life, give you resolve, and bring light to your issues and circumstances. I pray this will help define some of your relationships and let go the dead weight. May it create a better understanding of yourself, your boundaries, and enable you to release toxic rituals, habits, and thought processes.

Most importantly, I pray that this book will enhance your relationship with Jesus Christ and induce a greater determination to read the word of God.

## *Writing in The Dark*

The Lord has given me a gift in writing. Writing was never something that I wanted to do. Since I'm being honest and transparent, reading was never something I was interested in. I could read but, my comprehension hindered me from understanding and retaining what I read. Overthinking was a problem. I was adding my own concepts and questions to things already finished. Listening and hearing was a challenge.

Here is a perfect example: The Lord told me to write a small book on Domestic Violence which would be turned into a testimonial play. The title is "Rhythms of Unheard Voices." Some of the things He told me to write I experienced myself. Some things I was grateful for that I never experienced. So, I wrote what I heard the Lord say. I was even introduced to some women who went through those terrible life altering ordeals. After completing it I was ready to share it with the world. I had such a hard time putting it out there or exposing what the Lord had given me. Some messages and poems from this book were absolutely, shocking, mind-boggling, thought-provoking, sad, and disturbing. Years went by and I became frustrated because I did not understand why He had given me an assignment that appeared stagnant. "Frustration should be an inspiration to change."

During that time in my life when I wrote this book, I was going through Domestic Violence that affected me mentally and emotionally. I finally asked my Pastor to go over the book and give me her opinion about it. I felt bad because I did not think that I needed someone to critique what the Lord had given me. *"Where there is no guidance the people fall, but in abundance of counselors there is victory."* **(Proverbs 11:14)** The Lord has placed people in our lives for good reasons. Sometimes we may see these people as hindrances or helpers. *"The way of a fool is right in his own eyes, but a wise man is he who listens to counsel."* **(Proverbs 12:15)**

My Pastor said, "Miriam you are taking your audience to a dark place. There needs to be some type of recovery." There it was the answer to why the book was at a standstill. There was no victorious ending to the situations that the women faced in my book. In my life at that time I was in the dark about my situation. How can I write about a victorious end when I wasn't living victoriously?

It was then that I realized I was still living as a victim, so how could I write about freedom? She was critiquing my book and unaware of how she ministered to my life's situation. That's why the book was not ready. I could not hear the victorious outcomes of the situations that the Lord has given me because I wasn't living victoriously. So, I went back over the stories and after praying I heard the victorious endings because of the position that

I was now in. I was in a toxic relationship which hindered or hid freedom. Since I got out of that relationship, I was now susceptible to hearing correctly. When the Lord gives you something it's for you first then others. I was so grateful in knowing that he knows the beginning and the end of our lives. The Lord is not going to set you up for failure. His reputation is on the line. He is not going to place you in something without an exit. Hence the phrase, "going through."

# *Labels*

The word "Label" is defined as a classifying phrase or name applied to a person or thing. Labels are used to define, excuse, uplift, tear down, refine, and to position. If you aren't sure who you are you can be quarantined by labels. You can be destroyed by labels. You can be tricked by labels. Labels can be used to prevent, permit, to separate, to explain status and to predict. Labels can humiliate or buildup.

Labels are placed on fences, billboards, animals, other barriers, and people. What labels have been placed on you? Have they hindered or helped you? Are you accepting the label? Are you exasperating your life trying to fit in a certain label? Are you leading a double life being one label in front of people and being another label personally? Are you a public success and a private failure? Are you wearing someone else's label? Are you forcing labels on others?

You are conceived in labels. You are called a fetus, then infant, toddler, child, tweens, teenager, adolescent, adult, and then senior. Between those labels are other labels like rich, poor, intelligent, entitled, and challenged.

Some parents push their labels on you so you can live out their lives instead of yours. Some parents label you with hereditary illnesses, habits, and diseases. Some children live their adult lives still trying to live up to a childhood label they will never fulfill because of "mommy or daddy's" false expectations. Some parents label you with their insecurities, past and present hurts, and abusive nature's. Some labels are good to hold on to. It is up to you to decide which ones to release, respond to, or accept.

The Lord has a purpose for your life. He does not care what the world has labeled you. The label "Child of God" carries phenomenal weight. The world will label you as an addict for certain things. They want you to call yourself one for the rest of your life. Hello, "my name is and I'm an addict." My friend, if you turn it over to Jesus, Deliverance can be forever. Whenever a problem or a celebration arises, and the first thing you think about is a: drink, a smoke, or a pill, please go to your nearest meeting. If you have a delivered mentality, any problem that arises can be placed in Jesus' hands. Lay your burdens, cast your cares, send your woes to Him. Let Him lighten your load. He really wants to help.

Saying, "Lord I need you," will cause an internal change that will cause an external obedience. Why receive a label from a world that picks which sins/wrongs are great and small? Not many meetings for liars, thieves, adulterers, and blasphemers! Jesus receives the sexual workers, murderers, pedophiles, alcoholics, those suffering from identity crisis, and so on. Jesus has called you, his child. Constant labeling can be discouraging but if you know who you are you walk in greatness.

*"But you are a chosen people, a royal priesthood, a holy nation, God's special possession, that you may declare the praises of him who called you out of darkness into his wonderful light."* **(1 Peter 2:9)** Being a Christian should be a lifelong label. In Ephesians 3:1 Paul called himself a prisoner of Jesus Christ. The world will deem you unusual because of your faith in a living God. You are not hyped, worried, or stressed about the things of this world. The world will deem you strange because of your joyfulness in mourning type situations. The world will consider you odd because of the favor and protection over your life.

The Lord has opened doors for you that you were not qualified for. The world is constantly at awe because of the mercy and grace applied in your life. You are still alive! You should have been dead a long time ago, but God. "You are not lucky, you are loved." The world has labeled Christians because of our belief in Jesus Christ; From the Virgin birth to Him rising from the grave!

Can you escape labels? No, but you have the power to accept and deny any label emotionally and mentally. Jealousy and envy will be revealed in family and friends whom you did not expect to. *"You are the light of the world. A city that is set on a hill cannot be hidden."* **(Matthew 5:14)** People will see you and notice something different. The enemy sees you also. Haters will arise and attempt to add negative labels or try to strip away the positive aspects in your life. Will you give in or walk on the firm foundation of assurance knowing who and whose you are? *"You are the salt of the earth. But if the salt loses its saltiness, how can it be made salty again? It is no longer good for anything, except to be thrown out and trampled underfoot."* **(Matthew 5:13)**

I claim strength and perseverance in your life; in Jesus name! I pray that the distractions are noticeable and that the Lord gives you wisdom and guidance to respond accordingly. Don't receive just any label. Shake off the negative labels, regrets, and stagnant circumstances that prevent growth and moving forward. Your shape, skin color, your health, (whether it's good or bad) your gender, and DNA was already mapped out. *"But even the very hairs of your head are all numbered."* **(Luke 12:7)** Changing your appearance to suit a carnal need serves no purpose when you fully understand this verse *"I praise you because I am fearfully and wonderfully made; your works are wonderful, I know that full well."* **(Psalm 139:14)**

Some may say easier said than done. Why stay bound? Why be susceptible to emotional abuse? Embrace freedom and it will embrace you! Are you having bitter thoughts and moments because of labels? Believe in Yourself! Believe in the strength of the Lord! Are you a little low on strength well? Those battles are not yours, they're the Lords. Any sin/label can be forgiven and stripped away. Come to Jesus and rest your mind. Accept that through Jesus you are a new creature. Try that label!

# *Lying/Masking*

"Liar, liar, pants on fire!" "That's a bold face lie!" "It's just a little white lie!" These are some phrases used to ease the tension and insecurity of telling or hearing falsehoods and fallacies. When the reality is, lying is lying. A lie has no size, color, or shape. ***"Therefore, rid yourselves of all malice and all deceit, hypocrisy, envy, and slander of every kind." (1 Peter 2:1)*** A lie is an untrue statement or impression meant to deceive; a deliberate intent to mislead. Other words to describe lying: deceitful, disingenuous, counterfeit, cunning, two-faced, imposturous, sneaky, subtle, indirect, false, sly, shifty, and treacherous! I could go on but, you get the point! Someone may ask, "How are you feeling today?" You respond great but you are not feeling great. Why lie?

People lie for entertainment, popularity, or to escape responsibility, fear and accountability. Remembering lies can be difficult and more lies are needed to help sustain the previous lie. Lies have ruined civilizations and relationships, and destroyed characters. *"For such people are not serving our Lord Christ, but their own appetites. By smooth talk and flattery, they deceive the minds of naive people."* (Romans 16:18) All that to gain worldly possessions and notoriety. False representation can only last for a time/season. Still, we lie and sleep well at night.

Why is telling or revealing the truth so bad? Check your fears, motives, and intentions! Why will the truth hurt you/others? Why have we become so used to "sparing feelings/lying." That enables, hinders, and covers up facts. If it doesn't look good to you, feel good to you, or if it is not for you; there are ways to express your opinions, status, or rights without lying. Who created this middle ground between "yes and no." Was it you or Satan? **"All you need to say is** simply 'Yes' or 'No'; anything beyond this comes from the evil one" (Matthew 5:37). The Lord clearly deals with "yes, no, or later." The word, "maybe," suggests another question! God does not deal in "gray areas." We create these areas and conditions of illusions to appease our human nature and carnal minds.

Get over yourself? Fact or fiction, cold or hot, right or wrong, and left or right; You may not like either one. That is no excuse to make up another way to comfort your emotional position. The truth can be challenging, enlightening, and provide an exit. It can also promote growth, reveal danger, and set you free. Jesus said, *"Ye shall know the truth, and the truth shall make you free."* **(John 8:32)** The Lord wants us to bask in the truth. Our point of view will always be short-sighted because of our inability to see everything. That's why depending on the omniscience of God makes sense. Running from the truth to be comforted in a lie sounds ridiculous but, many of us have done it for whatever reason.

Masking is more of a physical lie. Your mind uses it as a defense mechanism. It is basically pretending. Hiding from people in plain sight is so common it is alarming. You may wear certain clothes to hide visual bruises. You may look nice to hide emotional scars. Some thieves, alcoholics, murderers and such, do not dress to be noticed. You display happiness, but you are sad. You display security to conceal your insecurities. You seek to deter and distract people from the truth about yourself. These fears about being found out, shamed, and ostracized are not gifts given to you. They are bad ideas and strongholds meant to deter, or distract, and destroy strength, courage, stability, and intelligence. Families and societies have instilled this "hush-up" vice for generations to cover up sin.

In the Bible, the Pharisees and Sadducees were described as self-righteous and hypocritical people. ***"In the same way, on the outside you appear to people as righteous but, on the inside, you are full of hypocrisy and wickedness."* (Matthew 23:28)** They despised Jesus. He saw their true heart.

Bullies, control freaks, abusers, and narcissists have tricked people by hiding the truth. Some go to extremes to convince people that their lives are perfect, and all is well. *"... for the Lord seeth not as man seeth; for man looketh on the outward appearance, but the Lord looketh on the heart."* **(1 Samuel 16:7)** People attempt to hide depression, anxiety, psychosis, narcissism, insecurities, hatred, confusion, happiness, and habits from others. Some makeup themselves to hide physical and mental imperfections. Some downplay their capabilities and intelligence to fit into stagnant environments. Why dumb-down yourself to make others feel comfortable? What kind of intimidation are you under?

If you do not understand something, ask. Pretending to know will cause one lie to suit another. Carnally it may work for a time but, spiritually the Lord has given His people discernment (an ability to judge well), wisdom, and common sense. We see you! They see you!

God continually sees you!

People use devices, jobs, money, education, politics, religion, makeup, medication, and other people to shift the truth about themselves. These are also used, to hide imperfections, to adjust what is already present, to camouflage, and fool others. Are you really trying to convince yourself of something instead of others? Is it a means to encourage you or someone else? Is it a way to discourage others? Why is it for others? What do you need to prove to others? Is it worth changing your appearance to please others? Is it a covert operation to distract people from the truth? Who are you really fooling?

Hello! How are you? "I'm good," you say. Lies! Are people asking out of concern, or ritual? Do they really want to know about your well-being? Some people do not care. They are caught up in their own world. They ask you questions as a greeting. Are they pausing for a response? Do they really want to know what is going on with you? Do you really want to disclose what is going on? Being vulnerable is scary but lying is not the answer. Pretending is lying. Dressing up on the outside to distract people from the turmoil that is going on inside of you is lying to yourself. I am not saying if you feel bad dress that way. If you wish not to discuss how you feel, it is okay to say, "I do not want to talk about it, no, I do not feel well, or I will comment later." Take out time to tell the truth or respond correctly.

People live in beautiful homes with abusive people. You hear people say, "wow, I would have never guessed that was going on and I cannot believe that happened." Those statements come from being tricked or not being able to accept the truth. Adam and Eve tried to deceive God, but by covering up they exposed their lies about knowledge. If you feel compelled to lie, then you are admitting consciously or unconsciously that there is a problem that needs to be addressed.

People use pills, drinks, and other substances to elude, disguise, and forget truth and responsibility. They fear sobriety because they do not want to face adulthood. Those tactics do not solve problems; they evade them.

An excuse/lie does not redeem you. *"The Lord detests lying lips, but he delights in people who are trustworthy."* (Proverbs 12:22) The truth is, we all deal with insecurities on some level. Pretending that you do not is a delusion you decide to dwell in. You cannot be mad at those who have chosen to be secure in their flaws. I mean, you can be mad but, who cares! Living in lies can only be comfortable for a season. Exposure creates humility or hatred.

Take off those masks and reveal the you that glorifies God or be a victim always seeking validation, seclusion, isolation, or worldly heights. You will never please everyone. If your focus is on pleasing God, your goals and agendas will line up. Be content with the tools given you. The truth is always better than sacrificing your purpose, integrity, and faith!

# *Rules vs Relationship*

Rules are regulations that are understood. Rules are put in place to direct, control, deter, protect, prohibit, distract, create change, disengage, or promote order. Rules can be created to bring about peace. Rules can also be inserted to impose, expose, mitigate, and regulate.

Rules become a problem when people think that they don't apply to them. Rules become a problem when they promote hatred, racism, bigotry, and slavery. Rules have been changed, disfigured, dismounted, regurgitated, and misplaced to suit those who want control over certain aspects, subjects, dominions, kingdoms properties, and mindsets. Rules are put in place to restrain and maintain. Intelligence may not always play a part in creating these rules. Some rules have been conjured up because of ignorance, anxiety, selfishness, and fear.

As children, we are taught rules to pacify certain ethnicities, races, personal family values and dysfunctions. Rules are put in place for protection, cautionary and preventive measures. As we grow and develop, we make decisions to follow these rules, continue to pass down these rules, disobey these rules, change or delete these rules. We also must figure out which rules pertain to us and which rules don't. Some rules are age-related, some rules only apply to either men or women. The "Rule of thumb" was said to come from an English law that condoned a man who beat his wife with a stick no thicker than his thumb. Some rules are for the rich, some rules are for the poor. Some rules are for politicians. Some rules only apply to certain religions, clubs and cliques.

Some rules have the appearance of bringing comfort, but are really meant to degrade, control, and promote confusion. Some rules have become obsolete because of time and technology. Some rules have been changed because of compassion, empathy, and because of the toxic nature they stand for. Some rules have been put in place to undermine or condone traditions and ritualistic practices. Some rules have been instilled to satisfy petty agendas. Some have been created to dominate other cultures and communities. Wars have been fought because people broke rules or refused to abide by them.

Now, you should be more knowledgeable about the reasons for rules. Now you should be able to recall rules you are following for no reason and realize they serve no purpose; they are just a means of control. Now you should also understand what rules you need to embrace.

Whose rules do we follow, consider, or promote? It's been proven in history that man is always changing the rules. God's rules don't change. *"For I am the Lord, I change not"* **(Malachi 3:6)** God's rules are for all people, not particular set. **"There is neither Jew nor Gentile, neither slave nor free, nor is there male and female, for you are all one in Christ Jesus." (Galatians 3:28)** Man has manipulated, twisted, and redirected His Word to suit our carnal nature and circumstances. Man's double standards incite rebellion and chaos.

Places of businesses, churches, clubs, cliques, and organizations have their own rules. Even areas that you live in have rules. You must decide whether you are going to follow these rules. Breaking some rules can come with heavy consequences, fines, and penalties. Understanding why rules are put in place is very important. When you understand then you have a responsibility to decide whether you should follow or ignore the rules. Laws are systems of rules recognized in a particular region meant to regulate the actions of its members which can be enforced by penalties.

In the Old Testament, in the 20th chapter of the book of Exodus, the Lord gave Moses commandments (community mandated amendments) for the Children of Israel. In the New Testament Jesus said, *"... Therefore anyone who sets aside one of the least of these commands and teaches others accordingly will be called least in the kingdom of heaven, but whoever practices and teaches these commands will be called great in the kingdom of heaven."* (Matthew 5:17-19)

When entering the House of the Lord David said, *"Enter into his gates with thanksgiving, and into his courts with praise be thankful unto him and bless his name."* (Psalm 100:4) That can be difficult when you enter the doors after the world has beaten on you and you get verbally smacked with rules at the thresholds of the church. You can't wear this, and you can't wear that. Some utter tattoos and piercings are frowned upon so cover them up. Wow! I'm pretty sure you did not receive those additions to your body inside church. They were done in some shop, at home, or wherever.

Many people forgot where they come from. No one is perfect whether they go to church or not. *"For all have sinned and come short of the glory of God."* **(Romans 3:23)** No one has a testimony that states they were/are perfect. We are supposed to be compassionate people of God; but some people have been hurt, scarred, and damaged by so-called Christians and Saints of God.

Understand the difference between rules and relationship. Love the Lord because of who He is and not as a fearful rule! There is a church for you! *"Not forsaking the assembling of ourselves together, as the manner of some is; but exhorting one another: and so much the more, as ye see the day approaching."* **(Hebrews 10:25)** Please return, Jesus is waiting with open arms to love you, embrace you, console and comfort you.

Some rules are just common sense. Don't talk when the preacher is preaching. Bow your head and close your eyes when someone is praying it's not Biblical it's a man-made requirement. There is no scripture that mandates us to bow our heads and close our eyes when we pray. I understand that closing your eyes can help omit distractions. When you are out there in the world Evangelizing, I don't suggest closing your eyes. Being aware of your surroundings is important. The Word does say, ***"This, then, is how you should pray: "'Our Father in heaven, hallowed be your name..."* (Matthew 6:9)** If you feel safe enough to close your eyes and bow your head do so. If you're driving, I don't suggest it. Many people close their eyes and bow their head and their heart posture is offensive to the Lord. Bowing your head is another way to humble yourself to God. He knows if you're sincere.

Just because someone is not in your club, clique, or circle does not mean their ministry is less effective. ***"Do not stop him," Jesus said. "For no one who does a miracle in my name can in the next moment say anything bad about me, for whoever is not against us is for us."* (Mark 9:39-40)** If someone or something is causing you to feel condemned for anything that you have done, please note, that is not the Lord Jesus Christ!

Let's be clear, there is nothing you can ever do to deserve the love of Christ. He loves you no matter what you have done or who you are. Being taught to establish a relationship with the Lord is more essential, lasting, and important.

If you feel condemned, manipulated, and stagnant, when it comes to rules from so-called friends and family members, please note demonic spirits are at work. There is freedom in saying, no! There is freedom in making changes within yourself so that others will not be able to quarantine you with their rules. You must set boundaries for yourself. Teach people how-to treat you. Construct rules for you. I say construct because it may take time to understand what rules need to be in place to keep your frame of mind. Build them!

Decide to become self-aware. It is okay to seek help from a mental health provider. Preferably one who believes in the Gospel of Jesus Christ. Yes, Jesus can fix anything. He has also provided people with gifts and talents to be resources in your life. He will get the glory out of your life. Understanding why rules have been placed upon you can open your eyes and reveal the motives of others. This does not pertain to governmental environments. You are responsible for being a law-abiding citizen. *"... Then he said to them, "So give back to Caesar what is Caesar's, and to God what is God's." (Matthew 22:21)*

By the way, the Lord is aware of the politics in this world. *"Let everyone be subject to the governing authorities, for there is no authority except that which God has established. The authorities that exist have been established by God. Consequently, whoever rebels against the authority is rebelling against what God has instituted, and those who do so will bring judgment on themselves." (Romans 13:1-2)*

Let Jesus work in your life. Forming a bond with your creator will free you from the bonds of religious ploys and tactics. *"I have told you these things, so that in me you may have peace. In this world you will have trouble. But take heart! I have overcome the world."*

**(John 16:33)** Because Jesus has overcome the world, you can also!

What it takes for the Lord to get your attention could be different from how he got mines and others attention. Therefore a personal relationship is necessary. *"Remain in me, as I also remain in you. No branch can bear fruit by itself; it must remain in the vine. Neither can you bear fruit unless you remain in me. I am the vine; you are the branches. If you remain in me and I in you, you will bear much fruit; apart from me you can do nothing."* **(John 15:4-5)** If anything needs to be added, subtracted, or refined, Jesus will let you know. "Thy will be done!" The church should be praying for their change not yours.

If you trust in the Lord that means you claim Him to be *"...the author and finisher of our faith"* **(Hebrews 12:2)** This means that you trust his purpose for your life. When that family member/s rejects you, when that organization or clique will not receive you, when the one/s you love turn you down, see it as a release from something that was not going to be beneficial in your life. When you see rejection as a release from the unknown, you trust the Lord and move on because you accept that He knows what's best. Others intentions and motives could be those, "dangers that are not seen."

I know it may still hurt your feelings! Get over it! Can you depend on this earthly vessel which is unstable? It has been proven that you can't. Just remember or recall your past! **_For I know that good itself does not dwell in me, that is, in my sinful nature. For I have the desire to do what is good, but I cannot carry it out. For I do not do the good I want to do, but the evil I do not want to do—this I keep on doing. Now if I do what I do not want to do, it is no longer I who do it, but it is sin living in me that does it."_** **(Romans 7:18-21)**

Therefore a spiritual relationship is detrimental to your well-being. Jesus sees you as his own. You are a Child of the King. That should override anyone's opinion about you! What are the toxic relationships that have rules you need to be free of? If you do not know, ask Jesus. *"For everyone who asks receives; the one who seeks finds; and to the one who knocks, the door will be opened."* *(Matthew 7:8) "For I know the thoughts that I think toward you, saith the Lord, thoughts of peace, and not of evil, to give you an expected end."* **(Jeremiah 29:11)**

Remember, rejection is merely a release from certain people, places, and things that we do not understand. Recite this: "This release is for my good." When the Lord sends you on an assignment and they turn you away, consider this, they are not rejecting you. They are rejecting the one who sent you, Jesus! *"As you enter the home, give it your greeting. If the home is deserving, let your peace rest on it; if it is not, let your peace return to you. If anyone will not welcome you or listen to your words, leave that home or town and shake the*

***dust off your feet.*** **" (Matthew 10:12-14)**

Jesus was rejected by his own and He still focused on doing God's will. What rejection is keeping you off task? There are people, places, and things that the Lord deemed not for you. You forcing the issue is going against God's plans and feelings of rejection settle in along with resentment, sadness, and anger. Are you sure you trust His plans for you? Focus on a relationship in Christ and not the relativities of this world!

# *Those Caves and Islands*

A cave has been described as a hole or opening in a land formation. Some caves are dank, dark, and damp. Some caves are small without an exit. Caves are wide with an exit. Although, some may have an exit, the exit can be dangerous and seem like a maze.

Some exits can be seen from the entrance. The proverbial "light at the end of the tunnel" so to speak. Some caves have an exit but the location hasn't been pinpointed. Caves can be beautiful because of the structure and forms of the rocks and indigenous life-forms that depend on this light starved atmosphere. There are pills, therapy, and other resources to help you conquer this cave mentality. Self-realization comes into place when you realize your cave. Is your cave a trap or a moment for transformation? **"The thief comes only to steal and kill and destroy" (John 10:10)** People are aware of people in caves.

When you compare cave-like features to a mindset you quickly think of darkness, depression, sadness, pessimistic thoughts, and destructive mannerisms and attitudes. There are people who dwell in these cave-like mindsets. Hurt, bitterness, anger, and unresolved issues dwell in these dark places. Any life forms found in a cave are there because they can thrive in that atmosphere. Sometimes while trying to find an exit in this cave, you find others who are looking for an exit also. Others do not want to be noticed in a cave, so they torture themselves by ignoring their surroundings. They camouflage themselves in their caves to appear as their dark dwelling place. Focus! Sometimes comfort can bring on a complacent nature.

I watched a show where a person with a certain key was able to unlock the door to their mind and physically walk into it. They were also allowed to let others come and explore what was in their mind also. I thought to myself, this was very interesting. They came face-to-face with fear; they killed it and buried it. When they returned through the door from their mind, they had no fear. However, someone else knew where their fear was located (pay attention). Whatever they hesitated to say or act upon before was now said and done with bravery and confidence.

What is causing you to stay or dwell in a cave-like mentality? You might not consider it a cave. It might be small like a pothole. It might be as big as a place to live in. Whatever the size, must you occupy this type of space or stronghold? What has convinced you to want to spend too much time in this place? "But the prophet Gad said to David, *"Do not stay in the stronghold. Go into the land of Judah."* (1 Samuel 22:5) Do not stay in that cave. Get to a point of praise. Praise the Lord to shake off distress. Praise the Lord for His goodness. Praise the Lord and let gratefulness condemn sadness. Praise the Lord to bring light to darkness.

What emotions, events, realities, or people are you evading or hiding from? ***"His divine power has given us everything we need for a godly life through our knowledge of him who called us by his own glory and goodness. Through these he has given us his very great and precious promises, so that through them you may participate in the divine nature, having escaped the corruption in the world caused by evil desires." (2 Peter 1:3-4)*** An escape is possible!

In the Bible there are many instances where people came across certain circumstances and problems. The phrase or term "going through" suggests an exit. There is another term that's frequently used, "it comes to pass." That term suggests a time limit. Nothing comes to stay. ***"Heaven and earth will pass away, but my words will never pass away." (Matthew 24:35)***

Omniscience, omnipotence, being omnipresent are all qualities and attributes of Jesus Christ. He is the light of the world (find scripture about him being a light unto my path). The light exposes, heals, produces, and defends. Darkness covers, conceals, promotes, and can initiate death. Straying off the path of righteousness can bring you to a cave. Caves are also used as a form of protection or a pause. That entails a need for being rescued. Are you aware of the cave you are in now?

Even though the sun is healthy, night is still necessary. You adjust better when you have the tools within you to refuse the dark. You learn how to appreciate both the light and the dark. Clarity can be found in a cave. The lesson learned in the dark is appreciated in the light. When you understand that you hold the light of the world within you, responsibility comes forward and rests in accountability.

## *Islands*

Feeling alone and being alone are two different things. Yes, it takes courage to meet new people, places, and things. Exposing yourself, vulnerability, privacy, personal problems, and dysfunctions are things human beings deal with. Are you going to be a victim of fear? Do you have faith? If your answer is yes, then, you can't turn your faith off and on to suit your insecurities. Well, you can; and if so, I question your faith! If you just have faith in that light switch that you flick off and on, that alarm you set, even that key or button you push to start your car, and the elevator buttons you push to go up or down; I insist that you level-up!

What happened to faith in getting well, faith during trials and seemingly difficult situations? *"For by the grace given me I say to every one of you: Do not think of yourself more highly than you ought, but rather think of yourself with sober judgment, in accordance with the faith God has distributed to each of you."* **(Romans 12:3)** I encourage you to use and activate fully, the measure of faith begotten you.

John, a disciple of Jesus Christ, was placed on an island as a punishment because of his Christianity. It was called Patmos (Revelation 1:9). That's proof that your beliefs, goals, and values can place you in a situation having you feel like you are alone. If you think about an island and how it is surrounded by a body of water, you can take it to a different level. While John was in this situation, he did not take out time to describe his environment and the pros and cons of it. John stayed on task and listened to what the Lord said and wrote Revelations. He did not focus on him being physically alone because in his spiritual sight he was not alone because the presence of the Lord was always with him and speaking to him.

If you think that you are all alone, you are not alone. *"Then I said, I am cast out of thy sight; yet I will look again toward thy holy temple."* **(Jonah 2:4)** I challenge you to look again and, "see."

You are set apart and not alone. Some people in your circle can't go where you are headed in this season. The Lord knows who needs to be around when God puts you in or on another level. There is a time for everything. *"To everything there is a season, and a time to every purpose under the heaven"* **(Ecclesiastes 3:1)** Don't focus on the environment. Keep your heart posture and your mind set on things above. *"Set your affections on things above, not on things on the earth."* **(Colossians 3:2)** Your emotional and mental health depends on a point of view.

If you really think about what would have happened if John wasn't placed on that island, he would not have heard the Revelation of God. When you are feeling like you are alone, just humble yourself and tune in to what the Lord is trying to tell you. When the word Island is mentioned one could imagine beautiful waters and tropical settings. Thoughts of vacationing, peaceful environments and limited amounts of people also come to mind. Another viewpoint of an island could be seclusion, loneliness, withdrawal, sadness, and confusion.

There are times when being by yourself is necessary. If you think being around people 24/7 is pertinent maybe dealing with yourself is an issue. Quiet time, taking a break, and relaxing is a must for better emotional, mental, and physical health. If you don't agree then ask yourself why don't you want to be by yourself? What is it about you that you don't want to face? Why do you only feel validated, happy, or in control when others are around? Sitting in the dark, only communicating through social media, or attempting to cut yourself off from the world indicates a problem.

This is self-examination time. Time to face you and all the good and bad things about you. What do you like about yourself? What don't you like about yourself? Who makes you feel this way? Are you comparing yourself to others? Why do you feel as if you are better off by yourself? Who have you allowed in your space to make you feel inadequate, fearsome, and lonely? Everyone isn't the same. You should not base your whole existence or perception based on a person or even a few people that have hurt or disappointed you. There are more than seven billion people on earth. You haven't met all of them! So, if everyone has a pessimistic agenda when they meet you, are conniving liars, or are just draining entities is not healthy. Yes, there are people with those qualities and shame on them. There are also people who just want to be kind, friendly, and resourceful.

If you are constantly meeting negative people and find yourself in crazy relationships check yourself. Re-evaluate, reset, and rediscover yourself! Realigning and readjusting your boundaries and the people within your space is necessary when maturing and leveling-up. This time is precious, not sad. It is joyful and not worrisome. This is where Relationship makes another significant mark. The Lord will place us in an uncomfortable place where things that would normally distract us are not around. The Lord knows us perfectly. He knows what environments, circumstances, atmospheres, and situations, that need to encircle us just so we can listen to what He has to say. Consider it, time for God. "If your sight is on the Light then the world is dim. All you will see is Him!" This is where your eyes need to be focused and understand: *"Now faith is the substance of things hoped for, the evidence of things not seen."* (Hebrews 11:1) So what you see carnally is a mirage because spiritually the battles aren't yours, they are the Lords! You are never alone! **"... and, lo, I am with you always, even unto the end of the world. Amen." (Matthew 28:20)**

Straying off the path presented to you can alter your mindset. Let us just call it what it is: disobedience. Following instructions are an essential piece to this walk in Salvation. Feelings of isolation can come because of your decisions to rearrange what Jesus has ordained and you just do your own thing. Thank God there is mercy and grace located on these islands.

Some people, places, and things are only for certain seasons and levels in your life. Accept it and move forward or you could waste time and energy trying to carry dead weight. Extra weight causes more problems. "The Lord had said to Abram, *"Go from your country, your people and your father's household to the land I will show you."* (Genesis 12:1) Abraham still took his cousin Lot with him. This delayed Abraham and he had to get Lot out of trouble a couple of times.

Following the Lord's instructions, completely, matters. Depression and worry will rear their ugly heads when the path you choose is not the one planned or purposed for your life. This leads to more prayers that include: Why is my blessing being delayed? Why did this problem come up? Why can't I move forward?

It is your decision! Island or Inland? What are you willing to put up with? What is your "absolutely not."

# Life from A to V

This chapter explains the words that some people live under, go through, have been labeled as, and just have a hard time with. Have you defined your life with/or by using the following words? There is time to repent and change!

**Abandoned:** forsaken or rejection. Jesus loves you. He will never forsake you. He knows what's best. ***"... for he hath said, I will never leave thee, nor forsake thee." (Hebrews 13:5)*** If you depend on Him fully you will treat any rejection as a release. If someone rejects you, be happy that they don't want to be a part of your life. The Lord may be the only one who knows why that person should not be in your life. Trust and have faith that the father knows best.

Trying to force something that should not be can be dangerous.

**Abrupt:** hasty and quick. Making any decisions should include the Lord. *"In all thy ways acknowledge him, and he shall direct thy paths." (Proverbs 3:6)* Don't be quick in excluding Him. (Example) You made a hasty investment and a week later you get laid off. "Plans without God are unfinished business!"

**Absurd:** unreasonable or inappropriate. Using sound judgment can be detrimental in surviving. How you react to negativity matters! Tantrums are not appropriate at any age. *"Would God that we had died in the land of Egypt! or would God we had died in this wilderness!" (Numbers 14:2)* The Israelites complained when they could not get their way or see the vision of their Leader. A journey that was supposed to last a couple of weeks took forty years. "No," doesn't always mean never. It could mean not now or not that way. Sometimes a "yes," depends on how you handled a "no!"

**Abstracted:** displaying a lack in concentration. Racing thoughts can be controlled. ***"Thou wilt keep him in perfect peace, whose mind is stayed on thee: because he trusteth in thee."*** **(Isaiah 26:3)** What percentage of things do you worry about that you have no power to change? Your conversations will not be focused, and others will notice but, you will be the one more frustrated. Peace!

**Adamant:** refusing to change your mind. Being stubborn when it comes to change creates restrictions. ***"When I was a child, I spake as a child, I understood as a child, I thought as a child: but when I became a man, I put away childish things."*** **(1 Corinthians 13:11)** The Egyptians came to the realization that their slaves had left. Now, they thought, "how was anything going to get done?" They could not accept that change. They went after the children of Israel and drowned in the Red sea. They wanted to keep things as is! Change promotes growth and growth promotes change.

**Aggravated:** irritable and annoyed. It is so easy to let the world's woes bother you, if you stay carnal minded. *"If ye were of the world, the world would love his own: but because ye are not of the world, but I have chosen you out of the world, therefore the world hateth you."* **(John 15:19)** This world can leave a bad taste in your mouth. *"O taste and see that the Lord is good: blessed is the man that trusteth in him."* **(Psalm 34:8)** Jesus is a better flavor!

**Aggressive:** competitive or menacing. The Lord has given us, choice. When you are spreading the Gospel of Jesus Christ, jamming it down someone's throat is unnecessary. *"And whosoever shall not receive you, nor hear your words, when ye depart out of that house or city, shake off the dust of your feet"* **(Matthew 10:14)** They are not rejecting you. They are rejecting Him. Some aggression can be good, when it pertains to God's glory. Let the Lord refine it, reset it and reclaim it for His will. He knows who he created.

**Alarmed/Apprehensive:** feeling frightened or in danger. Who told you to be scared? *"For*

*God hath not given us the spirit of fear; but of power, and love, and of a sound mind." (2 Timothy 1:7)* The enemy wants you to stay stagnant and dormant. Let that scripture take a load off your mind and be free!

**Alone:** obtaining no participation from others or isolation. If God is everywhere how can you be alone? *"If I ascend up into heaven, thou art there: if I make my bed in hell, behold, thou art there"* **(Psalm 139:8)** Your flesh will have you thinking you are alone. Your spirit will tell you God is with you. Who will you believe? When you have an encounter with Jesus, change occurs. A challenge to change is implemented. Feelings of isolation can be caused by the environment you have chosen. *"And when he went forth to land, there met him out of the city a certain man, which had devils long time, and ware no clothes, neither abode in any house, but in the tombs."* **(Luke 8:27)**

When you carry a lot of baggage you are not aware that everyone can see the stress, fake smile, and your lies about being happy. Do not succumb to the tragedies in your past. When you decide to face your fears, let it be amongst the living. Be grateful you have a testimony of victory. Believe you've been forgiven. Jesus does not have you feeling condemned. He adjusts you to move on. Pray, and move forward.

**Aloof:** unfriendly and distant. There are people assigned to you whether you realize it or not. Some are not people! ***"Be not forgetful to entertain strangers: for thereby some have entertained angels unawares."* (Hebrews 13:2)** Whether others say it to your face or not; they know when you have good intentions or a bad agenda!

**Amateur/Average:** incompetent or unskilled at a particular activity. Average: ordinary or common. So, you do not think you can accomplish things? *"I can do all things through Christ which strengtheneth me."* **(Philippians 4:13)** The Lord has given you power to overcome obstacles triumphantly. ***"Behold, I give unto you power to tread on serpents and scorpions, and over all the power of the enemy: and nothing shall by any means hurt you."* (Luke 10:19)** Believe it and achieve it! Child of God you, are not less than! *"Nay, in all these things we are more than conquerors through him that loved us."* **(Romans 8:37)** He has provided within us His undefeated Spirit, a friend and consoler. *"But the Comforter, which is the Holy Ghost, whom the Father will send in my name, he shall teach you all things, and bring all things to your remembrance, whatsoever I have said unto you."* **(John 14:26)**

Jesus has been calling you great things. If you have not heard Him, get to that secret place to hear his pleasant thoughts about you. His greatness dwells within you! *"But we have this treasure in earthen vessels, that the excellency of the power may be of God, and not of us." (2 Corinthians 4:7)* Read Romans 8 when in doubt. You are good enough.

**Ambiguous:** doubtful or unclear. It is impossible and mind trembling when you attempt to live a double life. *"A double minded man is unstable in all his ways."* **(James 1:8)** "Living as a public success while behind closed doors you are feeling like a private failure will catch up to you." Are you living a lie? Why?

**Ambitious:** determined to succeed or having a strong desire. Ambition can be a good thing if you do not commit any sins to achieve your goals. Underlying agendas can creep up on you when you are too thirsty. ***"And, behold, one came and said unto him, Good Master, what good thing shall I do, that I may have eternal life?"* (Matthew 19:16)** The Rich man assumed that there was nothing to stop him from entering into heaven because he thought he was a "do gooder." ***"Jesus said unto him, If thou wilt be perfect, go and sell that thou hast, and give to the poor, and thou shalt have treasure in heaven: and come and follow me. But when the young man heard that saying, he went away sorrowful: for he had great possessions."*** (Matthew 19:21-22) Ambitions require sacrifices. The Disciples had goals at one time to be great. ***"Then there arose a reasoning among them, which of them should be greatest."*** **(Luke 9.46)** They were with Jesus a lot and still sought to be great. Their carnal sight overwhelmed the bigger picture. Jesus was going to be crucified. That was the ultimate shameful way of being put to death. They were quarreling over who was the best. As social media would say, SMH! (Shaking My Head).

**Antagonizing:** to motivate someone to be hostile. Are you playing the devil's advocate? *"Because Haman the son of Hammedatha, the Agagite, the enemy of all the Jews, had devised against the Jews to destroy them, and had cast Pur, that is, the lot, to consume them, and to destroy them."* **(Esther 9:24)** In that story Haman was hung by the gallows he had built for Mordechai. Causing discord and strife for any kind of gain will always backfire. Maybe not at that time but... *"Be not deceived; God is not mocked: for whatsoever a man soweth, that shall he also reap."* **(Galatians 6:7)**

**Antiquated/Antediluvian/Archaic:** prehistoric or outdated. Jesus is the son of the living God. The Gospel of Jesus Christ is true. *"Think not that I am come to destroy the* *law, or the prophets: I am not come to destroy, but to fulfil."* **(Matthew 5:17)** *"Jesus saith unto him, I am the way, the truth, and the life: no man cometh unto the Father, but by me."* **(John 14:6)** *"And Jesus came and spake unto them, saying, All power is given unto me in heaven and in earth."* **(Matthew 28:18)** Jesus is Lord! I challenge you to check your habits and religious rituals that are more aligned with rules and not relationship. Church hats, Collars and costumes are not biblical. You should be recognized by your works and walk; not your outfit or position. If you must announce or make your title known, think about what prevented people from automatically seeing it,

**Antisocial/Autonomous:** not interested in the company of others. Autonomous: functioning as an independent entity. You cannot operate wholly by yourself. You are important and are part of a bigger purpose. It requires comradery, like-minded people, and togetherness. Teamwork! You have meaning.

*"And those members of the body, which we think to be less honourable, upon these we bestow more abundant honour; and our uncomely parts have more abundant comeliness. For our comely parts have no need: but God hath tempered the body together, having given more abundant honour to that part which lacked. That there should be no schism in the body; but that the members should have the same care one for another."* (1 Corinthians 12:23-25) No matter how insignificant you feel, (which is just a bad idea), Jesus says you are important and necessary. Who do you believe? Let the haters hate!

**Anxious/Apprehensive:** to worry about something with an uncertain outcome. Nothing changes because you let it consume your mind! *"Be careful for nothing; but in everything by prayer and supplication with thanksgiving let your requests be made known unto God."* (Philippians 4:6) Place your worries and woes in the Lord's hands. *"Heaviness in the heart of man* *maketh it stoop: but a good word maketh it glad."* **(Proverbs 12:25)**

You cannot prevent or stop a tomorrow not promised. *"Therefore, I say unto you, take no thought for your life, what ye shall eat, or what ye shall drink; nor yet for your body, what ye shall put on. Is not the life more than meat, and the body than raiment? Behold the fowls of the air: for they sow not, neither do they reap, nor gather into barns; yet your heavenly Father feedeth them. Are ye not much better than they."* **(Matthew 6:25-26)**

**Apart:** being separated from another person or thing using time or distance. When you feel isolated the omnipresence of God should overwhelm you. *"Paul, a servant of Jesus Christ, called to be an apostle, separated unto the gospel of God."* **(Romans 1:1)** His eternal presence should comfort you. If not, why? What man can do better? You are separated for purpose. Hanging with the wrong crowd can hinder your goals, blessings, and answers from God. There are a host of angels encamped around you. Embrace that joy and love.

**Apathetic:** showing no interest or concern. These days people's interests and attention span lack patience and tolerance. *"But he, willing to justify himself, said unto Jesus, and who is my neighbour?"* **(Luke 10:29)** It's selfish to just be concerned about yourself. You are called to be a light in dark places. Be concerned about your territory that the Lord has given you dominion over.

**Arbitrary:** subject to your own will without restriction, wayward, or tyrannical. Your way or the highway, right? You say you will never change for no one! Can you really handle everything by yourself? Change brings on new responsibilities. What don't you want to answer to? Being vulnerable takes courage. Courage requires a sacrifice of emotions. *"For it is God which worketh in you both to will and to do of his good pleasure. Do all things without murmurings and disputing."* **(Philippians 2:13-14)** When you get tired of the world beating on you. When you accept His plan, He is waiting.

**Asinine:** foolish or unintelligent. If you are living by what others say, if you base your views through other eyes, if you stand firm on gossip and confusion, your foundation is sandy, weak, and unstable. Whether you accept it or not, gray areas do not exist. We compromise the Lord's words to suit unethical needs and wants. *"I know thy works, that thou art neither cold nor hot: I would thou wert cold or hot."* (Revelation 3:15)

**Assuming:** taking much for granted. Living with entitlement issues can be dangerous. Are you really that self-centered in thinking you can place your "all" in this world? *"Hopes placed in mortals die with them; all the promise of their power comes to nothing"* (Proverbs 11:7) What kind of confidence are you mounted in that has you thinking that you have all the time in the world to follow God's plan for your life. *"Whereas ye know not what shall be on the morrow. For what is your life? It is even a vapor* *that appeareth for a little time, and then vanisheth away."* **(James 4:14)** Being grateful coats your selfishness with clarity. Procrastinating dulls your understanding in moving forward.

**Atheist:** denying or disbelieving the existence of God. This mother earth, father sky, luck, superior energy, cards being dealt, sound like excuses and figments of the imagination. If you do not want to accept that someone loves you unconditionally, okay! *"Among whom also we all had our conversation in times past in the lusts of our flesh, fulfilling the desires of the flesh and of the mind; and were by nature the children of wrath, even as others. But God, who is rich in mercy, for his great love wherewith he loved us."* (Ephesians 2:3-4)

If you refuse to believe that no matter what you've done you can be forgiven, okay! *"For God so loved the world, that he gave his only begotten Son, that whosoever believeth in him should not perish, but have everlasting life."* **(John 3:16)** If you have chosen to go through life under your own understanding and you are secure and will not wait for nothing, okay! *"But they that wait upon the Lord shall renew their strength; they shall mount up with wings as eagles; they shall run, and not be weary; and they shall walk, and not faint."* (Isaiah 40:31)

If you wish to remain bound by worldly situations and circumstances, okay! *"Casting all your care upon him; for he careth for you."* (1 Peter 5:7) If you just want to live in fear, okay! *"There is no fear in love; but perfect love casteth out fear: because fear hath torment. He that feareth is not made perfect in love."* (1 John 4:8) If you have placed your hopes and dreams in only this world, okay! *"If in this life only we have hope in Christ, we are of all men most miserable."* (1 Corinthians 15:19) If you are angry and pouting because things did not go your way, okay! *"Be ye angry, and sin not: let not the sun go down upon your wrath."* (Ephesians 4:26)

If you do want to live knowing that the true and living God, the Almighty King, the Creator of all has chosen you to be a part of Him, okay! *"Ye have not chosen me, but I have chosen you, and ordained you, that ye should go and bring forth fruit, and that your fruit should remain: that whatsoever ye shall ask of the Father in my name, he may give it you."* **(John 15:16)** It's your choice to believe; but, whether you believe or not... *"Wherefore God also hath highly exalted him, and given him a name which is above every name: That at the name of Jesus every knee should bow, of things in heaven, and things in earth, and things under the earth; And that every tongue should confess that Jesus Christ is Lord, to the glory of God the Father."* **(Philippians 2:9-11)**

**Atrocious:** cruel or dreadful. Who or what has you dwelling in hurt, fear, hatred and disgust? The relationships you are in won't last or reflect positivity. Saul hated David because of jealousy and his own lack of self-esteem. *"And Saul saw and knew that the Lord was with David, and that Michal Saul's daughter* *loved him. And Saul was yet the more afraid of David; and Saul became David's enemy continually."* **(1Samuel 18:28-29)** I know love can make you feel vulnerable and uncomfortable but it's freeing, boundless, and good. Why dwell in negativity? *"Beloved, let us love one another: for love is of God; and everyone that loveth is born of God, and knoweth God. He that loveth not knoweth not God; for God is love."* **(1 John 4:7-8)** Bask in the joy of the Lord. *"Finally, brethren, whatsoever things are true, whatsoever things are honest, whatsoever things are just, whatsoever things are pure, whatsoever things are lovely, whatsoever things are of good report; if there be any virtue, and if there be any praise, think on these things."* **(Philippians 4.8)**

**Avenging:** to take vengeance, to get even or payback. *"To me belongeth vengeance and recompence; their foot shall slide in due time: for the day of their calamity is at hand, and the things that shall come upon them make haste."* **(Deuteronomy**

**32:35)** A lot of people are just living without empathy and have no clue about kindness and being neighborly. *"For they are a nation void of counsel, neither is there any understanding in them."* (Deuteronomy **32:28)** Forgive for relief! *"Recompense to no man evil for evil. Provide things honest in the sight of all men. If it be possible, as much as lieth in you, live peaceably with all men. Dearly beloved, avenge not yourselves, but rather give place unto wrath: for it is written, Vengeance is mine; I will repay, saith the Lord."* (Romans 12:17-19)

Stewing and brewing in how to get back at someone can backfire. Vengeance comes with relatives like bitterness, depression, anxiety, stress, and an unrepentant heart. *"A wrathful man stirreth up strife: but he that is slow to anger appeaseth strife."* (Proverbs 15:18) Living to avenge is not a good way to end a day or leave this earth. *"Let all bitterness, and wrath, and anger, and clamour, and evil speaking, be put away from you, with all malice: And be ye kind one to another, tenderhearted, forgiving one another, even as God for Christ's sake hath forgiven you."* **(Ephesians 4:31-32)** Victims must repent for the evil thoughts and words towards false accusers and abusers. There is no gray area. You never know when your life or another's will end.

After you realize you have been living your life in/as negative "A" words you should see the need for change. My prayer is that you live a Victorious life.

**Vantage point:** a beneficial perspective or viewpoint. Our point of view will always be limited. Since the Lord is eternal, be comforted in knowing that from His viewpoint you are good, safe, and worthy. Moses didn't think or see how he could be the person used by God to set the Israelites free. He focused on his insecurities and on the fact that he was a murderer. *"However, as it is written: What no eye has seen, what no ear has heard, and what no human mind has conceived the things God has prepared for those who love him."* **(1 Corinthians 2:9)** He was known as a friend of God. Your possibilities are endless in the sight of God.

**Valuable:** costing a high price or important. Jesus died for us. He took on all the sins of the world and was crucified. *"You were bought at a price. Therefore, honor God with your bodies" (1 Corinthians 6:20)* You are loved that much!

**Variant:** showing variety or diversity. As children of God we are not supposed to look the same. Our hearts, praise and worship should be one accord. We come from all aspects of life. He has given us differences. No two people are alike. He uses our peculiarities for His Glory. *"When morning came, he called his disciples to him and chose twelve of them, whom he also designated apostles." (Luke 6:13)* They were chosen because of their hearts not appearances.

**Vastitude:** vast or immense. Bask in the almighty and everlasting love and joy in Jesus. *"Your love, Lord, reaches to the heavens, your faithfulness to the skies. Your righteousness is like the highest mountains, your justice like*

**the great deep."** **(Psalm 36:5-6)** His love covers you also.

**Vaticinal**: identified by prophesy or prophetic. You are special. *"But you are a chosen people, a royal priesthood, a holy nation, God's special possession, that you may declare the praises of him who called you out of darkness into his wonderful light."* **(1Peter 2:9)** I see you walking on the runway of God's plan. "Strike a pose!"

**Veracious:** truthful or honest in content. Being truthful is freedom and there is a correct way to do it. *"Instead, speaking the truth in love, we will grow to become in every respect the mature body of him who is the head, that is, Christ."* **(Ephesians 4:15)** We are responsible for spreading the truth about Jesus.

**Verified:** documented or established. You have been approved as a child of God to spread the Gospel of Jesus Christ. *"You did not choose me, but I chose you and appointed you so that you might go and bear fruit— fruit that will last—and so that whatever* *you ask in my name the Father will give you."* **(John 15:16)**

**Vertical:** upright. When your relationship with the Lord is functioning all earthly woes and circumstances will fall into place. *"Set your minds on things above, not on earthly things."* **(Colossians 3:2)** "… and the things of the earth will go strangely dim."

**Vesture:** covers like a garment or clothing. When living on the side of victory, changes can be visually seen. You are covered in Jesus. *"I put on righteousness as my clothing; justice was my robe and my turban."* **(Job 29:14)** Now that is a beautiful outfit!

**Viable:** the ability to live, grow, and expand. This life is doable in Christ. *"But the Advocate, the Holy Spirit, whom the Father will send in my name, will teach you all things and will remind you of everything I have said to you."* **(John 14:26)** He has given us the tools necessary to succeed.

**Vial:** a small container. Be that container that the Lord wants to pour into. *"Whom he poured out on us generously through Jesus*

*Christ our Savior, so that, having been justified by his grace, we might become heirs having the hope of eternal life."* **(Titus 3:6-7)** Are you available?

**Vessel:** a hollow utensil used for holding contents. As you carry the Holy Spirit within you, every decision is complemented with the Love of God. *"If a man therefore purge himself from these, he shall be a vessel unto honour, sanctified, and meet for the master's use, and prepared unto every good work."* **(2 Timothy 2:21)** Carrying His messages of love, liberty, and relief. "What? know ye not that your body is the temple of the Holy Ghost, which is in you, which ye have of God, and ye are not your own" (1 Corinthians 6.19)? The Lord resides in you. What a feeling!

**Vibrant:** pulsating with energy. Are you happy about Jesus? *"Shout for joy to the Lord, all the earth. Worship the Lord with gladness; come before him with joyful songs."* **(Psalm 100:2)** Day-to-day situations can weigh you down mentally and emotionally. Let the Joy of the Lord lighten your load and move you forward!

**Vicarious:** taking the place of another thing or person. Thank you for intercessory prayer. *"In the same way, the Spirit helps us in our weakness. We do not know what we ought to pray for, but the Spirit himself intercedes for us through wordless groans. "...because the Spirit intercedes for God's people in accordance with the will of God."* **(Romans 8:26-27)** Someone stood in proxy for you and prayed. Hallelujah! Jesus stands before the Father daily; interceding for you.

**Victorious:** conquering and triumphant. Yes, you are more than a conqueror. *"But thanks be to God! He gives us the victory through our Lord Jesus Christ... Let nothing move you. Always give yourselves fully to the work of the Lord, because you know that your labor in the Lord is not in vain."* **(1 Corinthians 15:57-58)** You refuse to live life as a victim. Victory is your name! *"But thanks be to God, which giveth us the victory through our Lord Jesus Christ."* **(1 Corinthians 15.57)** Any circumstance facing you should be greeted with an "I win" mindset!

**Vigilant:** watchful and alert. Paying attention to your surroundings is smart. The young people have this saying. *"Stay woke!"* *"Be on your guard; stand firm in the faith; be courageous; be strong."* **(1 Corinthians 16:13)** Closed eyes can't see!

**Vindicated:** to defend against opposition or to clear from accusation. That is a hallelujah moment right there. Jesus died for your sins. You have been cleared from all wrong. Jesus took your place on the cross. *"For Christ also suffered once for sins, the righteous for the unrighteous, to bring you to God. He was put to death in the body but made alive in the Spirit."* **(1 Peter 3:18)** No condemnation!

**Vital:** indispensable or essential. You serve as an important part in the Kingdom of God. You have meaning, and worth. There is not another you. You are strictly designed for heavenly places. You have been through some things that will help another, get through. *"Come, see a man, which told me all things that ever I did: is not this the Christ? Then they went out of the city and came unto* *him."* **(John 4:29-30)** She shared her encounter with Jesus and a whole town was saved. You are a chain reaction. **Act** now!!

**Virtuous:** upright or morally excellent. You are God's wonderful creation. I see you carrying out the plan of God. *"For all the city of my people doth know that thou art a virtuous woman."* **(Ruth 3:11)** Bless You!

**Vivacious:** lively or spirited. Because He lives so do you. *"And if Christ be in you, the body is dead because of sin; but the Spirit is life because of righteousness. But if the Spirit of him that raised up Jesus from the dead dwell in you, he that raised up Christ from the dead shall also quicken your mortal bodies by his Spirit that dwelleth in you."* **(Romans 8:10-11)** You are alive!

**Vivid:** full of life or clearly perceptible. You are on fire for God. You are alive and free. *"So, if the Son sets you free, you will be free indeed."* **(John 8:36)** Your "Yes Lord is showing!

**Vivify:** to enlighten or sharpen. As you connect with like-spirited folks you touch and agree to the plan of God. *"As iron sharpens iron, so one person sharpens another."* **(Proverbs 27:17)** That is a servant mentality!

**Volitant:** engaged in the power of flight or active: You waited for the Lord in order, to move in purpose, purposely. *"But those who hope in the Lord will renew their strength. They will soar on wings like eagles; they will run and not grow weary; they will walk and not be faint."* **(Isaiah 40:31)** Soar in love! Soar faith! Soar in ministry!

# Footstools

A footstool is simply what it says. It is something under your feet. It can be an object for relaxation or used for elevation. Hallelujah! People let you know whether they are a help or hindrance. You just must pay attention and stay armored.

*"Therefore, put on the full armor of God, so that when the day of evil comes, you may be able to stand your ground, and after you have done everything, to stand. Stand firm then, with the belt of truth buckled around your waist, with the breastplate of righteousness in place, and with your feet fitted with the readiness that comes from the gospel of peace. In addition to all this, take up the shield of faith, with which you can extinguish all the flaming arrows of the evil one. Take the*

*helmet of salvation and the sword of the Spirit, which is the word of God."* **(Ephesians 6:13-17)** The Lord will fight the battles. You are required to stand firm on the foundations of God's word. Stand back and watch the Glory of the Lord with praises on your lips.

Haters will hate! That is their position and purpose. Jesus watches over you daily. His hand of protection is all around you. ***"Do not touch my anointed ones; do my prophets no harm."* (Psalm 105:15)** He is reachable. If you cannot seem to reach Him then place that anger, hopelessness, envy, doubt, and restlessness under your feet for a better view. You will be able to see clearly over the mountainous trials that keep you low.

It may seem like jealousy and misery are cornering you. It may look like distress is trying to clothe you. You may feel as if loneliness is blocking your view. You may see the enemy all around you. Spiritually I urge you to look again. ***"Don't be afraid,"* the prophet answered. *"Those who are with us are more than those who are with them."* (2 Kings 6:16)** Keep in mind that victory will always cover you!

Knowing that the Lord has got your back should fill your heart with joy, security, and confidence. Sit back, relax, and put your feet up!

# Take Up Thy Bed and Walk

The Bible speaks of a man who had an infirmity. For thirty- eight years he laid by a healing pool waiting for someone to place him in the water to be healed. *"When Jesus saw him lying there and learned that he had been in this condition for a long time, he asked him, "Do you want to get well?" (John 5:6)* Do *you* want to be healed?

How long will you sleep in stagnant thinking, stubbornness, faithlessness, anger, and hurt. This man laid in his excuses for a long time. How long have you been waiting for the Lord to move you out of a mood? What circumstance have you chosen to sulk in? What is the emotional or physical damage that has you feeling conquered, condemned, or paralyzed? *"The thief cometh not, but for to steal, and to kill, and to destroy: I am come that they might have life, and that they might have it more abundantly."* (John 10:10)

The enemy has devised weapons to steal our joy, kill our meaning, and destroy our relationship with Jesus. These weapons are personal and designed to fit your character to the tee. They are meant to distract, deter, and confuse you. The Lord Says, *"... no weapon forged against you will prevail..."* (Isaiah 54:17) The enemy's tactical use of delusion and fear has been defeated by the strategic plan on Calvary. Do you believe? *"The weapons we fight with are not the weapons of the world. On the contrary, they have divine power to demolish strongholds"* (2 Corinthians 10:4) So why have you given these problems dominion over your life?

Taking up your bed is a responsibility. Pick up what kept you complacent. Clean up after yourself. When you make a mess, clean it up! Do not leave it for someone else to clean up. You don't want anyone else laying in your mess. This entails accountability. This also involves faith.

You must believe in order to get up. This also means you play a part. You must believe that Jesus healed you. His part is healing. Your part is the getting up; that's proof that you believe. Sometimes we asked the Lord to deliver us from some things. Later we plead Lord, Lord when are you going to deliver me. He has delivered you but, in your lack of faith you don't believe that he did it. You don't have enough faith to step away.

Laying in a situation or circumstance too long can cause paralysis of the mind, goals, and purpose. Let's just say procrastination. Also laying there tells you that you have all day to do things. You do not! You are also assuming that you have tomorrow to do something. Tomorrow is not promised. Then, there's that saying; "Do not put off tomorrow what you can do today." That saying is not a biblical "word for word." Does it have to be biblical for you to follow it? Common sense plays a part in decision-making also! If this is sensitive for you, too bad. Get up! I'm encouraging you to level up, move forward, and continue.

*"I do believe; help me overcome my unbelief."* **(Mark 9:24)** Jesus understands when your faith might need a jumpstart. His grace and mercy are everlasting. It wasn't the bed that made the man sick. It was his location and mindset. The bed contributed in making him comfortable in his situation. What or who is keeping you comfortable in a bad position? *"For our struggle is not against flesh and blood, but against the rulers, against the authorities, against the powers of this dark world and against the spiritual forces of evil in the heavenly realms"* **(Ephesians 6:12)**

When you take an account of this wrestling, you realize that it cannot be fought physically. If you can't move for yourself, think about the others that are waiting for you or have been watching you. You are responsible for helping another, discipling others, and teaching people. Whether it be through testimony or encouraging words. You have an obligation and an environment that the Lord has given you authority over. Whether it is your family, co-workers, or friends. As you take up your bed you encourage another to take up theirs.

Jesus has healed you. You cannot stay in the place where you were. You were sick in that environment. Now you are well. Pack it up. It's time for you to go to a different destination and don't look back. Believe that you are capable through Jesus to rise and move on.

# New Garment

As we enter this last chapter there is a mandatory dress code. If you are not prepared to wear this new outfit, go back and reread the previous chapter. *"No one tears a piece out of a new garment to patch an old one. Otherwise, they will have torn the new garment, and the patch from the new will not match the old. And no one pours new wine into old wineskins..."* (Luke 5:36-37) This new outfit requires a certain state of mind. Old habits, dead weight, stinkin' thinkin' and an unsteady gait will not accommodate or match this garment for this season. A new attitude should match your new garment. You are on a royal assignment. *"But you are a chosen people, a royal priesthood, a holy nation, God's special possession, that you may declare the praises of him who called you out of darkness into his wonderful light."* **(1 Peter 2:9)**

This new garment requires maintenance; an upkeep with the Word of God, a daily inspection, and it's the only outfit that will keep you in the sight of God. *"I delight greatly in the Lord; my soul rejoices in my God. For he has clothed me with garments of salvation and arrayed me in a robe of his righteousness, as a bridegroom adorns his head like a priest, and as a bride adorns herself with her jewels"* **(Isaiah 61:10)** Now, that is an outfit for life!

www.miriamwbrice.com

CPSIA information can be obtained
at www.ICGtesting.com
Printed in the USA
BVHW091148150621
609530BV00013B/2635